WILD CATS

Leopards

Anne Welsbacher

ABDO Publishing Company

visit us at
www.abdopub.com

Published by Abdo Publishing Company 4940 Viking Drive, Edina, Minnesota 55435.
Copyright © 2000 by Abdo Consulting Group, Inc. International copyrights reserved in all
countries. No part of this book may be reproduced in any form without written permission
from the publisher.

Printed in the United States.

Photo credits: Peter Arnold, Inc.

Edited by Lori Kinstad Pupeza
Contributing editor Morgan Hughes

Library of Congress Cataloging-in-Publication Data

Welsbacher, Anne, 1955-
        Leopards / Anne Welsbacher.
        p. cm. -- (Wild cats)
        Includes index.
        Summary: Describes social, feeding, and hunting behaviors, as well
        as physical characteristics and life cycles of these big cats.
        ISBN 1-57765-088-3
        1. Leopard--Juvenile literature. [1. Leopards.] I. Title. II. Series:
        Welsbacher, Anne, 1955- Wild cats.
        QL737.C23W447   2000
        599.75'54--dc21   98-12652
                                                                     CIP
                                                                     AC

Contents

Wild Cats around the World

*T*he leopard is one kind of wild cat. Leopards live in Africa, Israel, parts of Asia, and India. Other big cats live in South America, Asia, and Mexico. Leopards live in more places around the world than other wild cats do.

Leopards have spots that help them blend in with the land around them. Some other wild cats have marks, too, such as stripes or spots.

Big cats are good hunters. They have sharp claws and teeth. They chase animals, catch them, and eat them.

Leopards are smaller than most wild cats. But they are the best at **adapting**.

Leopards also are the best climbers. They climb trees to stay away from danger. And they are the best **stalkers**.

Leopards live in many parts of the world.

Big Cat, Little Cat

Both big cats and little cats have whiskers. They use them like fingers, to feel their way along small spaces. Both can see clearly at night—better than people can!

Both big and little cats are good hunters. Most big and little cats can pull their sharp claws into their soft paws. They stretch them out to scratch or kill.

Most big cats like to be alone. Leopards like it most of all! They are very **secretive**. They stay hidden and live alone.

Most big cats roar. Leopards roar, or make a rasping sound. But house cats purr.

House cats lie with their tails curled up close. Most big cats stretch their tails out long. Leopards have very long tails. Leopards also clean themselves like house cats do.

Big cats and little cats are very graceful. They can jump and land without knocking things over. They can balance in high places, and squeeze into small spaces.

Leopards are very secretive.

A Closer Look

*L*eopards have spots all over their bodies. The spots on each leopard are a little different from all others.

Leopards have tan colored coats. Leopards that live in forests or jungles are darker than those that live in grasslands and plains.

Some leopards are black. They are called panthers. They have black spots on black fur. You can see the spots if you look very closely.

Leopards are about seven feet (two m) or longer, counting the tail. They are longer than a grown-up person is tall.

They are shorter than other wild cats. It would take about two leopards lined up to be as long as a tiger.

Leopards do not weigh as much as some of their bigger cousins, either. But they are very strong and fast. A leopard can catch a bird in the air with the swipe of one big paw!

Leopards have spots all over their bodies.

The Leopard at Home

*L*eopards can **adapt** to different places. They live in jungles, hills, plains, and deserts. They live on islands in the middle of lakes. They live in African forests.

The area and climate leopards live in is called their **habitat**. Because leopards live in many different kinds of places, they have many different habitats, too.

Leopards need water to drink, food to eat, and places where they can climb trees or hide.

Leopards live in a variety of habitats.

A Champion Climber

Leopards are the best of all cats at climbing. They are very **agile**.

Leopards climb trees to escape danger. They rest on branches all day long, and sleep on branches, too. They balance by hanging their legs down on either side of the branch.

Leopards hunt at night. They eat every few days. They carry their food up into trees to eat it.

Leopards do not like to fight with each other. They will avoid one another rather than fight. But sometimes a male leopard will fight to defend a female leopard.

Leopard cubs fight over food. They push and shove more than lion or tiger cubs. This is because leopards are loners. They take care of themselves.

Leopards are great climbers.

The Predator's Prey

Leopards are **carnivores**. They also are called **predators**. The animals they eat are called **prey**.

Leopards eat monkeys, antelopes, zebra, wildebeests, gazelles, wild pigs, African hares, peacocks, snakes, sheep, birds, and goats. They even eat porcupines! They also eat grasshoppers, beetles, and fruit.

Leopards hunt by getting close to an animal. The leopard springs forward and knocks down the animal with its strong big paws.

The leopard bites into the prey's neck. It squeezes the animal's throat until it cannot breathe. After killing an animal, the leopard carries it up into a tree. There it can eat the meat in the next few days.

A leopard attacking a gazelle.

Cat to Cat

*L*eopards like to be on their own. They do not like to be near other leopards or other animals.

Each male has its own **territory**. Leopard territories are about six square miles (15 sq km). That is about the size of a big lake.

There is only one male in each territory. But sometimes a female and a male will share part of their territories.

Leopards walk with their tails held high in the air. Their babies, called cubs, can see them above the grass.

Leopards make many sounds. They make a puffing or raspy sound to call their cubs. This sound is called **prusten**. Cubs also make high crying sounds to call for help.

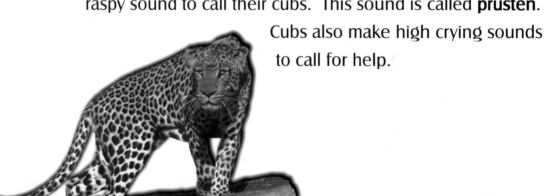

Leopards like to be alone.

Cat Families

*F*emale leopards raise their cubs alone. The leopard makes a safe home in a cave or in the branches of a tree. She gives birth to two or three cubs.

The cubs are born with spots. Their eyes are closed and they cannot walk. Their mother spends a lot of time with them. They **nurse** her for food.

After a few weeks, the mother leaves to go hunting. The cubs stay in their hidden home. If another animal finds them, it will try to eat them. So they stay as quiet and hidden as they can.

A leopard and her cub.

Growing Up

By the time they are about four weeks old, the cubs can eat the meat their mother brings back to the tree or cave. But they continue to **nurse** her, too.

The cubs practice hunting by chasing each other. They even chase their mother! The mother leopard knows these hunting lessons are important for her cubs.

By the time the cubs are one and a half years old, they can hunt by themselves. They are old enough to go out into the world on their own.

When her cubs are a year and a half or two years old, the mother leopard leaves. She finds another tree to live in. She **mates** again to have more cubs. At the age of two and a half, a young female leopard can mate and have her own cubs.

A leopard cub.

Glossary

Agile—able to jump and balance easily.

Adapt—to change when needed; for example, if a leopard can't find the food it likes to eat, it adapts and eats whatever food it can find.

Carnivore—an animal that eats meat.

Habitat—the area and climate that an animal lives in.

Mate—to join in a pair in order to produce young.

Nurse—baby leopards getting milk from their mother.

Predator—an animal that eats other animals.

Prey—an animal that is eaten by other animals.

Prusten—a sniffing, puffing sound made by leopards to call their cubs.

Secretive—hidden and alone, staying away from others.

Stalk—to sneak up on something.

Territory—an area or place where certain animals live; if others enter this area, the animal might fight or scare them off.

Internet Sites

Tiger Information Center
http://www.5tigers.org/
The Tiger Information Center is dedicated to providing information to help preserve the remaining five subspecies of tigers. This is a great site, with many links, sound, and animation.

The Lion Research Center
http://www.lionresearch.org/
Everything you want to know about lions is here. Lion research and conservation in Africa, information on lion behavior, and updates from researchers in the Serengeti about specific lion prides.

The Cheetah Spot
http://ThingsWild.com/cheetah2.html
This is a cool spot with sound and animation. Lots of fun information.

Amur Leopard
http://www.scz.org/asian/amurl1.html
This site links you to some great zoo spots. Very informative.

These sites are subject to change. Go to your favorite search engine and type in "cats" for more sites.

PASS IT ON

Tell Others What You Like About Animals!

To educate readers around the country, pass on interesting tips about animals, maybe a fun story about your animal or pet, and little-known facts about animals. We want to hear from you!

To get posted on the ABDO Publishing Company Web site, email us at "animals@abdopub.com"

Visit us at www.abdopub.com

Index

A

adapt 4, 10
Africa 4, 10
Asia 4

B

babies 16
black fur 8

C

carnivores 14
claws 4, 6
climb 4, 10, 12
coats 8
cubs 12, 16, 18, 20

F

female leopard 12, 18, 20
food 10, 12, 18
forest 8, 10
fur 8

G

grassland 8

H

habitat 10
home 18
house cat 6
hunters 4, 6

I

India 4
Israel 4

J

jump 6
jungle 8, 10

L

lion 12

M

male leopard 12
meat 14, 20
Mexico 4
mother 18, 20

P

panthers 8
paws 6, 8, 14

predator 14
prey 14
prusten 16
purr 6

R

roar 6

S

sleep 12
South America 4
spots 4, 8, 18
stalkers 4
stripes 4

T

tail 6, 8, 16
teeth 4
territory 16
tiger 8, 12
trees 4, 10, 12, 14, 18, 20

W

whiskers 6

24